Simply salads

Editorial Director: Brigitte Eveno

Art Directors: Guylaine & Christophe Moi

Production: Caroline Artémon

Editorial Assistant: Sylvie Gauthier

Editor: Sophie Brissaud

The publishers would like to thank Maïte Lapierre for her essential and thorough assistance.

© Hachette 2001/Hachette Livre (Hachette Pratique) 2003
This edition © 2004 Hachette Illustrated UK, Octopus Publishing Group,
2–4 Heron Quays, London E14 4JP

English translation by JMS Books LLP
(email: moseleystrachan@blueyonder.co.uk)
Translation © Octopus Publishing Group

A CIP catalogue for this book is available from the British Library

ISBN: 1 84430 056 0

Printed in Singapore by Tien Wah Press

Simply salads

Valérie Lhomme

Photographs by Iris L. Sullivan
Styling by Valérie Lhomme

HACHETTE Illustrated

Acknowledgements

For Margot, Tristan and Philippe

Many thanks to the following retailers for their loyal assistance: Quartz,
La Forge Subtile, Liwan, Blanc d'Ivoire, Palais Royale and Plastique.
Thanks also to Laurent, who once made me his 'Green Salad' and kindly
allowed me to publish the recipe here.

contents

summer salads

introduction

As soon as the weather gets warmer, the craving for salads begins. Vegetables look fresher, plumper, tastier; fruit is tantalizing, and herbs and spices are more plentiful and enticing. Salads are like a symbol of pleasant, warm days, and they must be savoured while the sun shines. They are easy to prepare and easy to enjoy, made with ingredients that have but a fleeting season – salads are a reminder that life and sunshine are there to be enjoyed. Cooking is not always required, though sometimes there's a thinly sliced sautéed baby artichoke or a sweet grilled pepper. Fresh herbs are plentiful and full of variety, to be used according to whim. Different types of salad herbs are abundant – purslane, rocket, baby spinach, and unusual Southeast Asian greens, as are edible flowers: rose petals and nasturtiums not only lift a salad with their flavour, but also appeal to the eye. Even simple green salads look more vibrant, with varying hues of green from the deep dark green of baby spinach to the palest of sea greens at the heart of a Little Gem lettuce. No matter the colour, the palette of summer salads is refreshing for the eyes and soul as well as the tastebuds. Satisfy three of the five senses in one go!

Rocket and rose petal salad

• Gently wipe the rose petals, making sure there are no 'visitors'.

• Wash and dry the rocket. Finely chop the shallots. Wash and dry the chervil and strip the leaves from the stems.

• For the vinaigrette: whisk together both the oils, vinegar and rose water. Season with salt and pepper.

• In a salad bowl, toss together the rose petals, rocket, chervil and shallots. Just before serving, toss with the vinaigrette.

Note: this is the perfect salad to serve with filo pastries filled with orange flower water-scented fromage frais.

Serves 4
Preparation: 15 minutes

2 handfuls rose petals
(pesticide free)
4 handfuls young, fresh rocket
2 shallots
½ bunch of chervil
1 tablespoon peanut oil
2 tablespoons fruity olive oil
1 tablespoon cider vinegar
1 tablespoon rose water
salt and pepper

Warm broad bean salad

• Shell the beans, then cook for 2 minutes in boiling, salted water. Drain and remove the skins while the beans are still warm. Set aside.

• Wash, dry and strip the leaves from the basil. Peel the garlic and remove any green shoots. Cook the garlic in boiling water for 1 minute. With a mortar and pestle, crush the garlic, then gradually add half of the olive oil and half the basil. Season with salt and pepper. Finely chop the shallots. Whisk together the lemon juice and remaining olive oil.

Serves 4
Preparation: 30 minutes
Cooking time: 6 minutes

2.3 kg (5 lb) broad beans
(about 1.1 kg/2 ½ lb shelled)
1 bunch of basil
3 garlic cloves
8 tablespoons olive oil
2 bunches of small fresh shallots
4 tablespoons lemon juice
salt and freshly ground pepper

• Warm the garlic and basil oil in a frying pan and add the beans and shallots. Cook gently for 4 minutes. Taste for seasoning and adjust if necessary. Add the lemon juice and olive-oil dressing and remaining basil leaves. Serve immediately.

Green and white asparagus salad with herbs

• Wash and dry the herbs and strip the leaves from the stems. Refrigerate until needed. With a vegetable peeler, cut the cheese into shavings.

• For the vinaigrette: whisk together the vinegar and 2 tablespoons of the olive oil with the grapeseed and pistachio oils. Season to taste.

• Trim the woody stems from the green asparagus, leaving only the tender tips. Peel the white asparagus and steam for 15 minutes; keep warm in the steamer. Heat the remaining olive oil in a frying pan, add the green asparagus and stir-fry over high heat until cooked. Season with salt and pepper.

• Toss the herbs in the vinaigrette dressing and divide between 4 plates. Top each with a mixture of green and white asparagus and the Pecorino shavings. Serve immediately.

Note: use Parmesan cheese if Pecorino is not available.

Serves 4
Preparation: 20 minutes
Cooking time: 20 minutes

½ bunch of chervil
½ bunch of chives
½ bunch of coriander
80 g (3 oz) Pecorino cheese
(with pepper if available)
2 tablespoons balsamic vinegar
4 tablespoons olive oil
1 tablespoon grapeseed oil
1 tablespoon pistachio oil
1 bunch of green asparagus
1 bunch of white asparagus
salt and freshly ground pepper

Courgette ribbons with toasted almonds

• Wash and dry the courgettes. With a vegetable peeler, slice the courgettes into thin ribbons. Arrange the ribbons in a dish and lightly season with salt.

• Wash and dry the radishes, and slice thinly.

• For the vinaigrette: whisk the oils and grapefruit juice together and lightly season. Toast the almonds under the grill, taking care they don't burn. Carefully combine the courgettes, radishes and vinaigrette. Sprinkle with the almonds and serve immediately.

Note: thinly sliced, raw smoked haddock is the ideal accompaniment for this salad; be sure not to oversalt the vinaigrette dressing.

Serves 4
Preparation: 15 minutes
Cooking time: 2 minutes

6 young, firm courgettes
1 bunch of radishes
3 tablespoons hazelnut oil
3 tablespoons fruity olive oil
3 tablespoons pink grapefruit juice
100 g (3½ oz) flaked almonds
salt and pepper

Serves 4
Preparation: 10 minutes
Cooking time: 20 minutes
Marinating time: 4 hours

1 teaspoon coriander seeds • 1 cos lettuce • 1 bunch of basil • 2–3 lemon thyme sprigs • 2–3 ordinary thyme sprigs • 2 garlic cloves • juice of 1 lime • 4 skinless, boneless chicken breasts (about 100 g/3½ oz each) • 7 tablespoons olive oil • 1 tablespoon walnut oil • 2 tablespoons lemon juice • salt and freshly ground pepper

Marinated chicken salad with cos lettuce

• Dry-fry the coriander seeds in a hot pan and coarsely crush.

• Wash and dry the lettuce and basil leaves. Break the lettuce leaves into pieces if too large.

• Strip the leaves from the basil. Tear half the leaves into pieces and refrigerate; finely chop the remaining leaves. Wash and dry all the thyme sprigs and strip the leaves from the stems. Peel the garlic, remove any green shoots, and crush.

• For the marinade: combine the lime juice, crushed coriander seeds, garlic, chopped basil, thyme and salt and pepper to taste in a shallow dish. Add the chicken breasts and coat with the marinade. Cover with clingfilm and refrigerate for 4 hours, turning occasionally so that the meat thoroughly absorbs the flavour.

• Preheat the grill. Cook the chicken breasts under the grill for 10 minutes each side, basting with the marinade.

• In a large bowl, toss together the lettuce, torn basil leaves and the oils. Add the lemon juice, season with salt and pepper, and mix well.

• Cut the cooked chicken lengthways into thin slices and serve with the salad.

Thai prawn and herb salad

- Remove the tough outer leaves from the lemon grass.
- For the prawns: remove the heads and peel up to the tails. Thread 3 prawns onto each of the 4 lemon grass stalks. Place the prawn kebabs in a shallow dish and season with 2 tablespoons kaffir lime juice and 2 tablespoons of the coconut milk. Toss with the ginger and chilli powder and allow to marinate for 15 minutes.
- Meanwhile, wash and dry the basil and purslane. Slice the spring onions.
- For the vinaigrette: whisk together 3 tablespoons of olive oil, the lime juice, spring onions and remaining coconut milk. Season with salt and pepper.
- Heat the remaining tablespoon of olive oil in a nonstick frying pan. Add the prawn kebabs and cook until pink, about 2 minutes, turning after 1 minute.
- Toss the basil and purslane with the vinaigrette and divide between 4 plates. Top each with a prawn kebab and serve immediately.

Note: kaffir limes and Thai basil are available in Southeast Asian shops.

Serves 4
Preparation: 20 minutes
Cooking time: 2 minutes
Marinating time:
15 minutes

4 stalks lemon grass
12 medium prawns
2 large kaffir limes (see note)
4 tablespoons coconut milk
3–4 teaspoons freshly grated
root ginger
1/2 teaspoon chilli powder
1/2 bunch of Thai basil
2 handfuls purslane, or spinach,
leaves
1 bunch of spring onions
4 tablespoons olive oil
juice of 1 lime
salt and freshly ground pepper

Roasted pepper and spiced feta salad

• Preheat the grill. Wash the peppers and arrange in a shallow flameproof dish. Grill until charred, turning regularly to cook on all sides. Remove the peppers and set the dish aside. Place the peppers in a plastic bag, seal tightly and allow to stand for 15 minutes.

• Peel the garlic cloves, remove any green shoots and crush. Halve the cherry tomatoes. Wash and dry the lemon thyme and strip the leaves. Deglaze the flameproof dish with the balsamic vinegar, then stir in the oil, lemon thyme, garlic and cherry tomatoes. Season to taste.

• Cut the feta into small cubes. Put each of the spices and dried herbs in separate dishes. Coat one-third of the feta cubes in paprika, one-third in turmeric and the rest in herbs.

• Remove the peppers from the bag, cut in half over a bowl to catch the juices, peel off the skins and cut the flesh into slices. Return the slices to the flameproof dish and add the pepper juices. Mix well and allow to stand to marinate for 30 minutes at room temperature. Serve with the feta and toasted slices of crusty bread.

Serves 4
Preparation: 30 minutes
Cooking time: 15 minutes
Marinating time:
at least 30 minutes

2 red peppers
2 yellow peppers
2 garlic cloves
12 cherry tomatoes
2 lemon thyme sprigs
2 tablespoons balsamic vinegar
4 tablespoons olive oil
salt and freshly ground pepper

• For the spiced feta:
200 g (7 oz) feta cheese
1 tablespoon paprika
1 tablespoon turmeric
2 tablespoons dried Herbes de Provence

Handy hints
for summer

Springs brings a bounty of fresh vegetables, new cheeses, herbs and tender young salad leaves. These freshly sprung and delicate ingredients require gentle treatment and respect. The first rule is not to overload them with heavy, creamy dressings. Citrus juice can easily replace vinegar in many dressings. It is best not to toss salads too far in advance; just before serving is perfect.

The Italian way to dress rocket is to first toss it in oil to coat the leaves, then the vinegar is added. This protects the leaves from the acidity of the vinegar so they stay fresh and crispy.

Use shallots, garlic, spring onions and herbs with abandon. Choose whole heads of lettuce that look fresh and crisp whenever possible, but you can use prepacked salad leaves as a standby. New packaging techniques have improved the flavour immensely.

• To add variety to dressings, use flavoured oils instead of ordinary. Divide 1 bottle of olive oil between 3 or 4 smaller bottles and flavour each with one of the following: 1 blanched rosemary or thyme sprig, red chillies, and a cinnamon or fennel stalk. Allow to stand for 1 week before using as you would ordinary olive oil.

• If tender, young leaves have wilted, refresh them in a large bowl of ice cold water. Spin dry gently, then place in a plastic bag and put in the vegetable compartment of your refrigerator.

• Take advantage of the warm weather to serve salads at every meal, adding prawns, cheese or dried fruit for accent. A little Parmesan, a handful of toasted pine nuts, a few leaves of fresh, crisp red leaf lettuce, and some rocket or basil are all that's needed for a delicious salad. Absolute freshness and quality ingredients are vital to the success of any dish that is served without cooking.

Marinated sardine salad

• Rinse the sardine fillets under cold running water and gently pat dry, Arrange in a shallow dish, skin-side down and drizzle over the lemon juice. Salt lightly and allow to marinate for 15 minutes.

• Meanwhile, wash and dry the spring onions and chives. Chop the spring onions into 4-cm (1½-in) long strips and snip the chives with scissors. Slice the red onion.

• Put a few spring onion strips on each of the sardines and roll up to enclose. Place in a shallow dish and sprinkle with chives and red onion. Whisk the vinegar and oil together and pour over the sardines. Cover with clingfilm and place in the refrigerator to marinate for 30 minutes.

• Serve with slices of toasted country bread or steamed new potatoes.

Serves 4
Preparation: 30 minutes
Marinating time:
15 minutes
Chilling time:
30 minutes

8 small fresh sardines, filleted
4 tablespoons of lemon juice
2 bunches of spring onions
1 bunch of chives
1 red onion
2 tablespoons sherry vinegar
5 tablespoons olive oil
fine sea salt and pepper

Green salad

• Trim the fine green beans. Steam all the vegetables for 3 minutes or until just tender, then plunge immediately into ice water to refresh and prevent from overcooking.

• Wash, dry and strip the leaves from the coriander.

• For the vinaigrette: whisk the lime juice and oil together, finally adding the fine sea salt and Szechuan pepper.

• Drain the vegetables and pat dry in a tea towel. Remove the outer skin from the broad beans, if preferred. Toss together the peas, broad beans, green beans and coriander. Add the vinaigrette dressing and gently mix to coat.

• Serve with a little coarse sea salt on the side and with slices of toasted baguette rubbed with fresh ginger.

Serves 4
Preparation: 30 minutes
Cooking time: 3 minutes

300 g (11 oz) fine green beans
450 g (1 lb) shelled peas
450 g (1 lb) shelled broad beans
1 bunch of coriander
3 tablespoons lime juice
6 tablespoons fruity olive oil
$\frac{1}{2}$ teaspoon fine sea salt
$\frac{1}{2}$ teaspoon Szechuan pepper
1 baguette, sliced and toasted
1 thumb-size piece of fresh root ginger, peeled
coarse sea salt, for serving

Serves 4
Preparation: 20 minutes
Cooking time: 40 minutes

1.4 kg (3 lb) climbing French beans (about 800 g/1³/₄ lb shelled) or 3 x 400 g (14 oz) cans flageolet or cannellini beans • 1 courgette • 2 tomatoes • 2 garlic cloves • 6 tablespoons olive oil • 1 thyme sprig • 1 shallot • 100 ml (3¹/₂ fl oz) dry cider • 500 g (18 oz) clams • 2 tablespoons cider vinegar • 1 bunch of coriander • salt and freshly ground pepper

Climbing French bean salad with sautéed clams

• Shell the beans if using fresh; rinse and drain canned beans. Wash and dry the courgette and tomatoes and cut into small pieces. Peel the garlic, remove any green shoots and crush.

• Heat 1 tablespoon of the olive oil in a pan and add the garlic, courgette and tomatoes. Add the beans, thyme sprig and 125 ml (4 fl oz) water. (If using canned beans add only the thyme and water at this stage; add the beans almost at the end to warm through.) Season with salt and pepper, then cover and simmer gently for 15–20 minutes. Add more water if necessary during cooking.

• Peel and finely chop the shallot. Heat 1 tablespoon of the olive oil in a pan, add the chopped shallot and cook until translucent. Add the cider, raise the heat and boil for 2 minutes, then add the clams. Cook until the shells open, being careful to discard any that remain un-opened. Take from the heat and remove the clams from their shells.

• For the vinaigrette: whisk the remaining oil and the cider vinegar together. Season with salt and pepper. Pour half of the vinaigrette onto the clams and mix well.

• Wash and dry the coriander and strip the leaves from the stems. When the bean mixture is cooked, remove from the heat and stir in the coriander. Allow to cool. Toss with the remaining vinaigrette and serve with the clams.

Spiced chickpea salad

Serves 4
Preparation: 10 minutes
Marinating time: at least
1 hour

**2 large ripe tomatoes • 1 red onion •
1 garlic clove • 4 tablespoons olive oil
• 1 tablespoon sesame oil • 2 tablespoons lemon juice • 1 teaspoon good-
quality harissa • ½ teaspoon ground
cumin • 1 x 400 g (14 oz) can chickpeas
• 1 bunch of coriander**

• Place the tomatoes in a bowl and pour over boiling water to cover. Leave for 1–2 minutes. Drain, cut a cross at the stem end and peel off the skin. Remove the seeds and finely chop.

• Finely chop the red onion. Peel the garlic, remove any green shoots and very finely chop. Mix both the oils and the lemon juice together and add the harissa, cumin, onion and garlic.

• Rinse and drain the chickpeas and toss with the chopped tomatoes. Stir in the spiced vinaigrette, cover and allow to marinate for at least 1 hour.

• Wash and dry the coriander, strip the leaves and toss with the salad just before serving.

Serves 4
Preparation: 30 minutes
Cooking time: 15 minutes
Marinating time: at least 1 hour

2 red peppers • 2 yellow peppers • 2 green peppers • 1 bunch of coriander • 2 garlic cloves • 1 thumb-size piece of fresh root ginger • 2 shallots • 2 tablespoons balsamic vinegar • 2 tablespoons wine vinegar • 1 tablespoon tapenade (black olive paste) • 8 tablespoons olive oil • 12 slices country bread, toasted • a few black olives • salt and freshly ground pepper

Grilled marinated peppers with ginger

• Preheat the grill. Wash the peppers and arrange in a shallow flameproof dish. Grill until charred, turning regularly to cook on all sides. Remove the peppers and set the dish aside. Place the peppers in a plastic bag, seal tightly and allow to stand for 15 minutes.

• Wash the coriander and strip the leaves. Peel the garlic, remove any green shoots and finely chop. Peel and grate almost all of the ginger. Finely chop the shallots.

• For the vinaigrette: whisk together the vinegars and the tapenade. Stir in the oil, garlic, grated ginger, shallots and season to taste.

• Take the peppers from the bag, cut in half over a bowl to catch the juices, remove the skins and cut the flesh into slices. Deglaze the flameproof dish with the vinaigrette and stir in the coriander leaves. Add the pepper slices and pour in the pepper juice. Mix well, cover and allow to marinate for at least 1 hour.

• Serve warm, with toasted bread slices that have been rubbed with the remaining ginger. Garnish with a few black olives.

Cucumber salad with mint

- Wash, dry and coarsely chop the mint. Halve the lime. Carefully remove the zest from one half and finely chop; squeeze the juice from both halves. Peel the garlic, remove any green shoots and finely chop.
- In a large bowl, combine the yogurt, mint, garlic, lime zest and olive oil. Season to taste and set aside.
- Wash the cucumber. With a vegetable peeler, remove the skin in alternating strips to obtain a striped pattern. Cut in half lengthways and scoop out the seeds in the middle with a small spoon. Cut into thin, half-moon slices. Toss with the yogurt dressing.
- Serve chilled as a starter, or to accompany grilled meat.

Note: if you make this dish in advance, make sure you taste for seasoning before serving. Cucumbers exude liquid as they stand and this will dilute the flavour.

Serves 4
Preparation: 15 minutes

½ **bunch of mint**
1 **lime**
1 **garlic clove**
500 g (18 oz) **tub plain yogurt
(preferably not set)**
4 **tablespoons olive oil**
1 **cucumber**
salt and freshly ground pepper

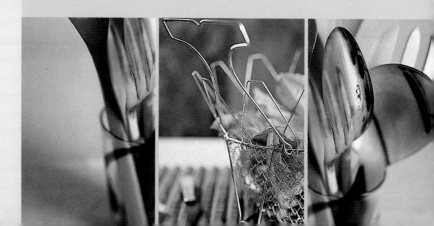

Pink salad

• Peel all the beetroot. Roughly chop one beetroot and purée in a food processor, then force the puree through a sieve to extract all the juices. Mix the beetroot juice with the vinegar and both the oils. Season with salt and pepper. Cut the remaining 3 beetroot into cubes and toss with the beetroot dressing. Set aside.

• Thinly slice the red onions. Wash and dry the basil leaves. Wash the radishes and cut into thin slices. Add the onions, basil, and radishes to the beetroot and toss well. Sprinkle with pink peppercorns and refrigerate until serving.

Serves 4
Preparation: 15 minutes

4 large cooked beetroot
2 tablespoons wine vinegar
3 tablespoons sunflower oil
2 tablespoons olive oil
2 red onions
12 red basil leaves
1 bunch of radishes
1 teaspoon pink peppercorns
salt and freshly ground pepper

Artichoke and rocket salad

• Wash and dry the rocket.

• For the vinaigrette: whisk 4 tablespoons of the olive oil with the saffron and balsamic vinegar. Season with salt and pepper. Using a vegetable peeler, slice the cheese into shavings.

• For the artichokes, remove the tough outer leaves, trim the stems and the tips of the leaves and cut in half. Thinly slice the halves, coating with lemon juice as you go to prevent them discolouring.

Serves 4
Preparation: 15 minutes
Cooking time: 5 minutes

4 handfuls rocket
6 tablespoons olive oil
pinch powdered saffron
2 tablespoons balsamic vinegar
80 g (2³/₄ oz) Gruyère or Beaufort cheese
8 small violet-tinged artichokes
4 tablespoons of lemon juice
80 g (2³/₄ oz) pine nuts
salt and freshly ground pepper

• Heat the remaining olive oil in a nonstick pan. When hot, add half of the artichokes and cook until golden and crispy, about 5 minutes. Season with salt and pepper. In another pan dry-fry the pine nuts.

• Toss the rocket, raw artichokes, pine nuts and vinaigrette. Divide between 4 plates, add the sautéed artichokes and top with the cheese shavings. Serve immediately.

Sea bream ceviche with peaches

Serves 4
Preparation:
20 minutes
Marinating time:
varies

½ vanilla pod
8 tablespoons olive oil
½ bunch of dill
½ teaspoon dill seed
2 ripe peaches
450 g (1 lb) very fresh sea
bream fillets (see note)
juice of 1 yellow grapefruit
juice of 2–3 limes
½ teaspoon pink peppercorns
salt and freshly ground pepper

• Split the vanilla pod. Heat the oil in a pan over low heat. When hot but not smoking, add the vanilla pod, remove from the heat and allow to stand to infuse for 30 minutes.

• Meanwhile, wash and dry the dill, then snip with scissors. Crush the dill seed.

• Cut the sea bream fillets into very thin slices. Arrange in a shallow dish and pour over the grapefruit and lime juice. Season with salt and pepper. Allow to stand for 5 minutes, then add the crushed dill seed and pink peppercorns. Refrigerate until needed. (The citrus juice will 'cook' the fish, which will turn opaque when ready, but do break open a piece to check. The timing depends on the texture and quality of the fish.)

• When the fish is ready, thinly slice the peaches. Drain off the marinade, pour over the vanilla oil, add the peach slices and the snipped fresh dill.

Note: this is delicious served with a tomato and dill salad, and some slices of toasted country bread. You can use other firm, white fish in place of the sea bream, such as cod, halibut or monk fish.

Serves 4
Preparation: 30 minutes
Chilling time: 1 hour

3 bunches of flat leaf parsley • 1 bunch of mint • 80 g (3 oz) cracked wheat (bulgur wheat) • 2 lemons • 1 small lettuce • 200 g (7 oz) ripe tomatoes • 1 large onion • 6 tablespoons olive oil • pinch of salt • freshly ground pepper

Tabbouleh

• Strip the leaves from the parsley and mint, then wash and pat dry.

• Pour some warm water over the cracked wheat and allow to stand for 15 minutes or as packet instructions.

• Wash and dry the lettuce, then refrigerate until needed. Squeeze the juice from both lemons. Cut the tomatoes into small cubes. Finely chop the onion and season with the salt and 2 grinds of the peppermill. Finely chop the mint and parsley.

• Squeeze out the cracked wheat in your hands, leaving just moist grains. Place in a large bowl and toss in the parsley, mint, tomatoes and onion with the oil and lemon juice to taste.

• Taste for seasoning and adjust if necessary. Cover and refrigerate for 1 hour. Serve chilled, with the lettuce leaves.

Note: This tabbouleh will keep for 24 hours, tightly covered in the refrigerator.

Onion and date salad

• Peel and thinly slice all the onions. Stone the dates, quarter, and place in a large bowl with the sliced onions. Stir in the walnut and olive oils, sugar, half the cinnamon and the lemon juice. Mix well and season to taste with salt. Cover with clingfilm and place in the refrigerator for 1 hour.

• Sprinkle with the remaining cinnamon and serve immediately.

Serves 4
Preparation: 10 minutes
Chilling time: 1 hour

Note: A fresh, young goats' cheese makes an ideal accompaniment.

2 sweet onions
2 bunches of large spring onions
12 Tunisian dates
1 tablespoon walnut oil
2 tablespoons olive oil
1 teaspoon sugar
1 teaspoon ground cinnamon
(freshly ground if possible)
1 tablespoon lemon juice
salt

Lebanese bread salad

• Wash and dry the herbs, spinach if using, and lettuce. Strip the leaves from the parsley and mint. Wash and peel the cucumber and slice into rounds. Wash the radishes and cut into rounds. Thinly slice the onions. Slice the tomatoes into small sections. Peel the garlic, remove any green shoots, and crush.

• Whisk together the garlic, dried mint, olive oil, lemon juice, vinegar, sumac and a pinch of salt.

• Toast the bread until crisp and golden, then break into pieces.

• In a large bowl, toss together the vegetables, herbs and vinaigrette. Add the bread pieces, garnish with a few olives, and serve immediately.

Note: sumac can be found in Middle Eastern speciality shops.

Serves 4
Preparation: 20 minutes

½ bunch of flat leaf parsley
½ bunch of mint
1 handful purslane, or spinach, leaves
1 small red-leaf lettuce
1 cucumber
½ bunch of radishes
2 red onions
300 g (11 oz) ripe tomatoes
1 garlic clove
½ teaspoon dried mint
6 tablespoons olive oil
1 tablespoon lemon juice
1 tablespoon wine vinegar
½ teaspoon ground sumac (see note)
2 Lebanese style flat breads, or pitta breads
a few olives, to garnish
salt

Nasturtium toasts with orange flower butter

• Remove the butter from the refrigerator and leave to soften. Carefully wash and dry the nasturtiums. Refrigerate until needed.

• Lightly toast the bread slices. Stir the orange flower water into the softened butter, then spread thinly on each bread slice and top with a slice of ham.

• Lightly toss the flowers with the oil and a mere pinch of salt and pepper. Arrange on top of the bread and ham slices and serve.

Serves 4
Preparation: 10 minutes

60 g (2 oz) unsalted butter

16 orange and yellow nasturtium blooms

4 large slices of rustic, country-style bread, about 1 cm ($\frac{1}{2}$ in) thick

1 teaspoon orange flower water

4 thin slices Parma ham

1 teaspoon olive oil

salt and freshly ground pepper

winter salads

Recipe list

introduction

Salads may seem ordinary, but they don't have to be. There is so much more to salads then just some tomatoes, cucumber slices and a few lettuce leaves tossed with dressing. With just a little creativity and imagination, they can be transformed to the extraordinary. More than any other dish, the art of salad making is in the combination of ingredients. The dressing is simply an enhancement and should never mask the true flavours. Autumn and winter are a time for well-contrasted ingredients, where the tastes and textures complement and complete one another, with the occasional surprise ingredient. There should be a good mix of tender and crisp, such as crunchy toasted almonds and winter fruits (apples and pears), with strong aromatic vinegars like balsamic or sherry, and a hint of bitterness from earthy winter vegetables. Warm, substantial salads can easily become a main dish. When creating medleys, try mixing colours for an eye-pleasing result, or stick to a single colour for an equally impressive presentation. Splash out on luxury ingredients like truffles, wild mushrooms, scallops or foie gras. Salad making is an art and the results should be attractive and vivid, bringing a little light and warmth to cold winter days.

Warm cabbage and leek salad with eggs

• Trim the leeks and rinse under cold running water. Wash the cabbage leaves, pat dry and cut across each leaf to form thin slices. Coarsely grate the cheese or cut shavings with a vegetable peeler. Peel and crush the garlic clove, removing any green shoots.

• For the vinaigrette: stir together the soy sauce and vinegar. Add both the oils, the crushed garlic, sesame seeds and salt and pepper to taste. Mix well and allow to stand.

Serves 4
Preparation: 30 minutes
Cooking time:
15 minutes

8 thin leeks
1 small green cabbage, outer leaves removed
100 g (3½ oz) 'aged' Mimolette cheese
1 garlic clove
1 tablespoon soy sauce
1 tablespoon sherry vinegar
1 tablespoon sesame oil
3 tablespoons olive oil
1 tablespoon toasted sesame seeds
4 fresh eggs, at room temperature
1 baguette, with sesame seeds if available
salt and freshly ground pepper

• Steam the leeks and cabbage slices in separate pans for 15 minutes.

• Bring a pan of water to the boil, add the eggs and cook for 5 minutes. Transfer the eggs to a bowl and rinse under cold running water to prevent overcooking. When cool, shell and cut in half or quarters lengthways.

• Put the still-warm leeks and cabbage in a bowl and toss with the vinaigrette. Top with the eggs and cheese and serve with thin slices of the baguette.

Potato salad with fresh and smoked salmon

- The day before serving, cut the fresh salmon fillet into 4 equal pieces and remove any bones. Cut across the slices of smoked salmon to form 1.5-cm ($1/2$-inch) strips. Peel the carrot and cut into rounds. Cut the onion into thin slices. Crush the juniper berries. Wash the bay leaf and thyme.
- Put the fresh and smoked salmon pieces in a dish with a lid. Add the carrot, onion, juniper berries, bay leaf, thyme and coriander seeds. Pour over the grapeseed and olive oils and mix to coat the ingredients. Cover and refrigerate overnight.
- On the day of serving, steam the potatoes for 15 minutes or until tender. Keep warm.
- Remove the salmon pieces from the marinade and serve with the potatoes and a little of the marinade, seasoned with a generous sprinkling of sea salt and pepper.

Note: For extra crunch, serve this dish with a simple green salad.

Serves 4
Preparation: 15 minutes
Cooking time:
20 minutes
Marinating time:
24 hours

200 g (7 oz) fresh salmon fillet
200 g (7 oz) smoked salmon, thickly sliced
1 carrot
1 red onion
4 juniper berries
1 bay leaf
1 thyme sprig
$1/2$ teaspoon coriander seeds
200 ml (7 fl oz) grapeseed oil
100 ml (3$1/2$ fl oz) olive oil
450 g (1 lb) baby new potatoes
sea salt
freshly ground pepper

Chicory and blue cheese salad

• Preheat the oven to 180°C (350°F) gas mark 4.

• For the garnish: melt the butter, brush over the crêpes and bake in the oven for 5 minutes, until crispy. Set aside.

• Trim the chicory, and separate all the leaves, discarding any blemished ones. Wash and pat dry gently. Refrigerate until needed.

• Coarsely chop the pistachios and walnuts. Cut the cheese into small cubes and quarter the dried apricots.

• For the vinaigrette: combine the oils, vinegar and mustard until blended. Season with salt and pepper.

• In a large bowl, toss together the chicory leaves, cheese and apricot pieces. Pour over the vinaigrette and mix carefully. Dry-fry the pistachio and walnut pieces and sprinkle over the salad. Serve immediately, with pieces of crispy crêpes.

Serves 4
Preparation: 15 minutes
Cooking time: 5 minutes

3 heads chicory
50 g (1³/₄ oz) shelled unsalted pistachios
50 g (1³/₄ oz) walnut pieces
125 g (4 oz) blue cheese, such as Fourme d'Ambert
4 plump dried apricots
3 tablespoons sunflower oil
1 tablespoon walnut oil
1 tablespoon sherry vinegar
¹/₂ teaspoon whole-grain Dijon mustard
salt and pepper

• **For the garnish:**
20 g (³/₄ oz) butter
2 buckwheat or ordinary crêpes

Watercress, baby spinach and wild mushroom salad

Serves 4
Preparation:
20 minutes
Cooking time:
30 minutes

450 g (1 lb) wild mushrooms, such as chanterelles
½ bunch of watercress
2 handfuls baby spinach
1 shallot
6 tablespoons olive oil
2 tablespoons aged wine vinegar
2 pinches curry powder
2 tablespoons walnut oil
1 tablespoon plain flour
100 g (3½ oz) Parmesan cheese, freshly grated
salt and freshly ground pepper

• Wipe the mushrooms and trim the stems. Gently wash and dry the watercress and spinach. Finely chop the shallot.

• In a frying pan, heat 3 tablespoons of the olive oil, add the shallot and cook over low heat until soft. Add the mushrooms, season with salt and pepper and cook over medium heat for 20 minutes, or until the liquid is completely evaporated.

• For the vinaigrette: whisk the vinegar and curry powder together in a small bowl. Whisk in the remaining olive oil and the walnut oil. Season with salt and pepper and allow to stand.

• In a small bowl, combine the flour and Parmesan. Spread a thin layer of this mixture in a nonstick frying pan and cook over low heat for 2 minutes without browning. When it becomes lacy, carefully remove from the pan and lay over a bottle or rolling pin to give it a curved shape as it cools and hardens.

• Toss the spinach and watercress with the vinaigrette. Add the mushrooms, top with pieces of the Parmesan *tuile* (thin biscuit) and serve.

Serves 4
Preparation: 20 minutes
Cooking time: 12 minutes

**20 firm, young chanterelle mushrooms • 16 fresh scallops • 5 tablespoons olive oil •
1 teaspoon balsamic vinegar • 1 tablespoon hazelnut oil • pinch of grated nutmeg •
1 teaspoon Tamari soy sauce • salt and pepper • fine sea salt**

Hot and cold scallop salad

• Wipe the mushrooms, trim off the bottom of the stems and separate the caps from the stems. Finely chop the stems.

• Rinse the scallops and pat dry. Cut 8 of the scallops in half horizontally, to obtain 16 thin discs and set aside. Cut the remaining scallops across into thin slices and arrange in a single layer in a dish. Sprinkle lightly with sea salt, pepper, 3 tablespoons of the olive oil and the balsamic vinegar. Cover and allow to stand in the refrigerator.

• Thinly slice the mushroom caps. Season with salt and pepper, then toss with the hazelnut oil, nutmeg and soy sauce.

• Heat the remaining olive oil in a pan. When hot, add the chopped mushroom stems and cook over high heat until browned. Remove from the pan, season to taste and allow to stand sandwiched between 2 plates to keep warm.

• In the same pan, add the scallop discs and cook for 2 minutes. Season with salt and pepper.

• Divide the raw, marinated scallop mixture between 4 plates. Add the mushroom caps, cooked scallops and cooked mushroom stems. Serve with a little sea salt on the side.

Black salad

• Peel the potatoes and cook in boiling, salted water until tender, 20–30 minutes depending on their size.

• Finely chop the shallots.

• For the vinaigrette: mix the tapenade, balsamic vinegar and half the shallots in a small bowl. Stir in 4 tablespoons olive oil and season to taste with salt and pepper. Set aside.

• Wipe the mushrooms. Heat the remaining olive oil in a nonstick frying pan. Add the remaining shallots and cook until just soft, then add the mushrooms. Cook for 30 minutes, stirring occasionally, until the liquid is completely evaporated. Season with salt and pepper.

• Slice the potatoes and mix with the olives. Add the mushrooms, toss with the vinaigrette and sprinkle with the sesame seeds. Serve immediately.

Serves 4
Preparation: 15 minutes
Cooking time: 1 hour

450 g (1 lb) black potatoes
2 shallots
1 tablespoon tapenade (black olive paste)
2 tablespoons balsamic vinegar
6 tablespoons olive oil
450 g (1 lb) mushrooms (horn-of-plenty, if possible)
50 g (1³/₄ oz) small black olives, pitted
1 teaspoon black sesame seeds
salt and pepper

Cooked carrot salad with oranges

• Slice the carrots into thin rounds. Squeeze the juice from 2 of the oranges.

• Heat the butter in a pan, when melted and foaming, add the carrots, orange juice, ground cumin, cinnamon and salt and pepper to taste. Simmer, covered, until the carrots are tender, about 15 minutes. Allow to stand until cool.

• Wash, dry and remove the coriander leaves from the stems. Refrigerate until needed. Juice the remaining ½ orange.

• For the vinaigrette: whisk the two oils together in a small bowl. Add the lemon and orange juice and season. Dry-fry the almonds.

• Mix the cooled carrot mixture with the coriander leaves. Toss with the vinaigrette, sprinkle with the toasted almonds and cumin seeds and serve immediately.

Serves 4
Preparation: 15 minutes
Cooking time:
15 minutes

2 bunches of thin, young carrots
2½ oranges
30 g (1 oz) unsalted butter
½ teaspoon ground cumin
3 pinches ground cinnamon
1 bunch of fresh coriander
3 tablespoons olive oil
1 tablespoon walnut oil
4 tablespoons lemon juice
75 g (2¾ oz) flaked almonds
½ teaspoon cumin seeds
salt and freshly ground pepper

handy hints
for winter

To get the most from your cooking, it's essential to observe the seasons. Each one brings with it a wide variety of ingredients: vegetables, cheeses, fruits and herbs that are culinary inspirations in themselves. For autumn and winter salads, experiment with combining hot and cold ingredients, such as cooked vegetables with raw vegetables. The only rule is to toss the salad at the last minute so that the warm ingredients don't make the raw vegetables and lettuce leaves go limp or soggy. Be sure to have a good supply of different oils and vinegars to hand, kept in a cool, dark place to preserve their freshness. Lighten the flavour of olive oil by mixing it with grapeseed oil. A few drops of sesame, walnut or hazelnut oil will lift a vinaigrette out of the ordinary. Use different spices in place of black pepper, such as chilli or mixed peppercorns. Even more than the main ingredients, oil, vinegar and spices will lend variety to your winter salads.

• Choose ingredients that correspond to the place your salad will have in the meal. If you begin lunch with a salad, go easy on the beans, bread and meats and opt for vegetables, cheese shavings, herbs and seafood. If salad is the main course, then be sure to use some warm ingredients and include carbohydrates, such as root vegetables.

• Keep it simple and don't use too many different ingredients. Three or four should be plenty and will allow for more creativity when it comes to making the vinaigrette. A salad should never be a bunch of ingredients just thrown together haphazardly; choose thoughtfully, as you would for a main dish.

Curried lentil salad

• Rinse the lentils under cold running water. Slice the carrots into rounds. Slice one of the onions into rounds. Tie the herbs for the bouquet garni together with string.

• Heat 1 tablespoon of the oil in a pan, add the onion, 1 tablespoon of the curry powder and the cinnamon and cook until golden. Add the carrots, bouquet garni, lentils and cold water to cover (about 3 times their volume in weight). Bring to the boil, then lower the heat and simmer for 30 minutes. Add a little salt just before the end of the cooking time.

• Wash the parsley and pat dry. Coarsely chop and set aside.

• For the vinaigrette: whisk together both the vinegars and the remaining curry powder. Finely chop the remaining onion and add along with the remaining oil. Season with salt and pepper.

• When the lentils are cooked, drain off any excess liquid, discard the bouquet garni and place in a bowl. Toss while still warm with the chopped parsley and the vinaigrette. Serve immediately.

Serves 4
Preparation: 15 minutes
Cooking time:
30 minutes

400 g (14 oz) Puy lentils
4 carrots
2 red onions
1 bouquet garni (sprig of thyme, bay leaf, few stalks of parsley)
5 tablespoons olive oil
1½ tablespoons curry powder
½ teaspoon ground cinnamon
1 bunch flat-leaf parsley
1 tablespoon balsamic vinegar
1 tablespoon wine vinegar
salt and freshly ground pepper

Thai-style beef salad

- Preheat the grill. Brush a little sesame oil on the rack of a grill pan and grill the beef fillet for 3 minutes on each side, depending on the thickness.
- Deseed and finely chop the chillies. Finely chop the lemon grass, onion and shallot. Coarsely chop the peanuts. Wash the aubergines, remove from the stalk and cut each in half. Wash and dry the mint leaves.
- In a small bowl, mix together the sunflower oil, lime juice, nam pla, sugar and chopped chillies.

- Cut the beef fillet into thin slices and place in a bowl. Add the aubergines, onion, shallot, lemon grass and lime juice mixture. Cover with clingfilm and allow to stand at room temperature for 30 minutes.
- Before serving, sprinkle with mint leaves and the chopped peanuts. Accompany with white rice.

Note: bunches of green Thai aubergines can be found in Southeast Asian markets or speciality shops. You can also substitute small violet-white tinged aubergines.

Serves 4
Preparation: 10 minutes
Cooking time: 6 minutes
Marinating time: at
least 30 minutes

1 tablespoon sesame oil
300 g (11 oz) beef fillet
4 green chillies
½ stalk lemon grass
1 onion
1 shallot
50 g (1¾ oz) peanuts
3 bunches green Thai aubergines
(see note)
6 mint leaves
4 tablespoons sunflower oil
2 tablespoons lime juice
1 tablespoon nam pla
(fish sauce)
½ teaspoon sugar

Serves 4
Preparation: 15 minutes
Cooking time: 40 minutes
Marinating time: 2 hours

2 rosemary sprigs, stripped • 4 tablespoons honey • 4 tablespoons soy sauce • 600 g
(1¼ –1½ lb) pork spare ribs • 1 teaspoon sherry vinegar • 1 teaspoon icing sugar •
1 teaspoon nam pla (fish sauce) • 1 tablespoon sesame oil • 3 tablespoons sunflower
oil • 2 handfuls curly endive (frisée) • 2 tart dessert apples • 1 tablespoon toasted
sesame seeds • salt and freshly ground pepper

Honey-rosemary spare ribs with sweet and sour greens

• Wash and chop the rosemary leaves. In a small bowl, stir together the honey, 3 tablespoons of the soy sauce and the rosemary. Cut the ribs into sections with 2 bones each. Brush the rib sections all over with the honey mixture, cover and refrigerate for 2 hours.

• Preheat the grill. Cook the ribs under the grill until well browned and cooked, turning halfway through cooking.

• For the vinaigrette: whisk together the vinegar, sugar, nam pla and remaining soy sauce. Whisk in both the oils and season with salt and pepper.

• Wash and dry the curly endive. Peel the apples and cut into matchsticks. Combine the endive and apples in a bowl. Toss with the vinaigrette and sesame seeds. Serve immediately with the spare ribs.

Potato and Reblochon cheese pancakes with chicory salad

Serves 4
Preparation: 30 minutes
Cooking time: 30 minutes

1 Reblochon cheese • 2 thyme sprigs •
700 g (1½ lb) waxy potatoes, preferably
Charlotte • 100 g (4 oz) unsalted butter •
2 heads of chicory
For the vinaigrette: 4 tablespoons olive
oil • 2 tablespoons walnut oil • 2 tablespoons balsamic vinegar • salt and
freshly ground pepper

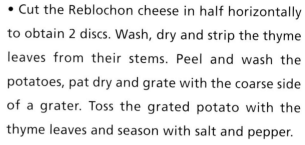

• Cut the Reblochon cheese in half horizontally to obtain 2 discs. Wash, dry and strip the thyme leaves from their stems. Peel and wash the potatoes, pat dry and grate with the coarse side of a grater. Toss the grated potato with the thyme leaves and season with salt and pepper.

• Cook in two batches, using two 20-cm (8-in) nonstick frying pans. Divide the potato mixture into 4 equal portions. Melt 25 g (1 oz) of the butter in each pan. When foaming, add one-quarter of the potato mixture in a thin circle and top with one of the cheese rounds. Cover with another quarter of potato mixture and spread to the edges of the cheese round and push down lightly. Cook over low heat for 10 minutes. Using a plate, turn the potato pancakes over, divide the remaining 50 g (2 oz) butter between each pan. When it begins to foam return the potato pancakes and cook on the second side for 15–20 minutes more.

• Meanwhile, separate the chicory leaves, wash and pat dry.

• For the vinaigrette: whisk oils and vinegar together and season. Just before serving, toss the chicory and vinaigrette and serve with the potato-cheese pancakes.

Serves 4
Preparation: 15 minutes

4 handfuls lamb's lettuce (mâche) • 12 tarragon leaves •
3 large cooked beetroots • 3 oranges • 2 tablespoons
sherry vinegar • 4 tablespoons olive oil • 1 tablespoon
hazelnut oil • 100 g (3½ oz) sliced or chopped hazelnuts •
salt and pepper

Beetroot and orange salad

• Wash the lamb's lettuce and gently pat dry. Wash and dry the tarragon leaves. Peel the beetroot. Purée one beetroot in a blender or food processor, then force through a sieve to extract all the juice. Reserve the juice. Squeeze the juice from 1 orange.

• For the vinaigrette: whisk together the vinegar, 1 tablespoon of the beetroot juice and 1 tablespoon of the orange juice. Whisk in the oils and season with salt and pepper.

• Peel the remaining 2 oranges and slice carefully between the membranes to loosen and extract the segments. Cut the remaining 2 beetroot into cubes. Dry-fry the hazelnuts.

• In a large bowl, gently mix together the lamb's lettuce, tarragon, orange segments and beetroot. Toss with the vinaigrette dressing, sprinkle with the nuts and serve immediately.

Mixed bean salad with warm vinaigrette

• Drain and rinse the beans. Place in a large bowl, add the bay leaf, rosemary and thyme, season with salt and pepper and set aside. Finely chop the shallot.

• For the vinaigrette: whisk together the vinegar, shallot and all the oils. Warm in a small pan.

• With a vegetable peeler, slice the Parmesan into shavings. Wash and dry the chives and snip with scissors.

• Cut the ham into strips and cook in a pan until warmed through

• Remove the herbs from the beans, add the warm vinaigrette and chives and toss well. Serve garnished with the crisped ham slivers and Parmesan shavings.

Serves 4
Preparation: 10 minutes
Cooking time:
10 minutes

2 x 400 g (14 oz) cans mixed beans (kidney, flageolet, cannellini, pinto etc.)

1 bay leaf

1 rosemary sprig

1 thyme sprig

1 shallot

3 tablespoons balsamic vinegar

3 tablespoons sunflower oil

1 tablespoon walnut oil

2 tablespoons olive oil

100 g (3½ oz) Parmesan cheese

1 bunch of chives

200 g (7 oz) cured Italian ham, thinly sliced

salt and freshly ground pepper

Marinated prawn salad

• Remove the prawn heads. Wash the fennel and celery, trim and slice thinly.

• Peel the garlic, remove any inner green shoots and finely chop. Place in a small bowl with 1 tablespoon of the olive oil, $\frac{1}{2}$ tablespoon of the sesame oil, the turmeric and the chilli powder. Mix well, then brush over the prawns. Cover and refrigerate for 30 minutes.

• For the vinaigrette: combine the remaining oils, lime juice, Tamari sauce, poppy seeds and season with salt and pepper. Place the fennel and celery in a bowl and toss with the vinaigrette.

• Heat a frying pan and cook the marinated prawns until cooked through, about 4 minutes. Serve immediately, with the fennel and celery salad.

Serves 4
Preparation: 20 minutes
Cooking time: 4 minutes
Marinating time:
30 minutes

16 small raw prawns
1 fennel bulb
1 celery heart
4 garlic cloves
3 tablespoons olive oil
1 tablespoon sesame oil
$\frac{1}{2}$ teaspoon ground turmeric
pinch chilli powder
2 tablespoons grapeseed oil
juice of $\frac{1}{2}$ lime
1 tablespoon Tamari soy sauce
1 teaspoon poppy seeds
salt and freshly ground pepper

Curly endive salad with quails' eggs

• Wash and dry the curly endive and trim the outer, dark green leaves. Wash, dry and strip the tarragon leaves from their stems. Refrigerate until needed.

• Trim the rind from the bacon and slice into small strips.

• For the vinaigrette: whisk together the mustard and vinegar in a small bowl. Gradually whisk in 4 tablespoons of the oil until the mixture thickens. Season with salt and pepper.

• Heat the remaining oil in a nonstick pan. When hot, add the bacon strips and cook for 2 minutes. Crack open the quails' eggs and add to the pan, cook for a further 2 minutes.

• Toss the curly endive with the vinaigrette and divide between 4 plates. Arrange the bacon strips and quails' eggs on top. Sprinkle with tarragon leaves and serve immediately.

Serves 4
Preparation: 20 minutes
Cooking time: 5 minutes

1 head curly endive (frisée)
1 bunch of tarragon
4 rashers smoked bacon
1 teaspoon Dijon mustard
2 tablespoons wine vinegar
5 tablespoons sunflower oil
8 quails' eggs
salt and freshly ground pepper

Fig and foie gras salad

Serves 4
Preparation:
15 minutes

2 handfuls watercress
2 teaspoons sherry vinegar
1 teaspoon acacia honey
3 tablespoons olive oil
1 teaspoon truffle oil
3 plump dried figs
6 ripe purple figs
4 thick slices pâté de foie gras
(duck)
thin slices pain de campagne
(rustic country bread)
fine sea salt
freshly ground pepper

• Wash and dry the watercress, then trim the stems. Refrigerate until needed.

• For the vinaigrette: whisk together the vinegar and honey, then gradually whisk in both the oils. Season with salt and pepper

• Cut the dried figs into small cubes and slice the fresh figs into rounds.

• Toss the watercress with the vinaigrette and divide between 4 plates. Top each with equal amounts of fresh and dried figs and place a slice of foie gras on each. Sprinkle with sea salt and a grinding of pepper. Serve with lightly toasted bread slices.

Serves 4
Preparation: 15 minutes
Cooking time: 4 minutes

1–2 radicchio heads • 1 fennel bulb • 1 bunch of chervil • 2 tablespoon balsamic
vinegar • ¹/₂ teaspoon five-spice powder • 1 teaspoon ground aniseed • 2 tablespoons grapeseed oil • 3 tablespoons olive oil • 2 dessert pears (comice, if available)
• salt and freshly ground pepper

Radicchio with pears, fennel and aniseed

• Separate the radicchio leaves, wash and gently pat dry. Trim the fennel and thinly slice. Wash and dry the chervil.

• For the vinaigrette: whisk together the vinegar, five-spice powder, half of the aniseed and season with salt and pepper. Whisk in the grapeseed oil and 2 table-spoons of the olive oil. Set aside.

• Preheat the grill. Halve and core the pears, then cut into thin slices. Brush with the remaining olive oil and sprinkle with the remaining aniseed. Sprinkle with a few grindings of pepper and grill for 4 minutes or until brown.

• Toss the fennel and chervil sprigs with the vinaigrette. Divide between 4 plates, top with the pear slices and serve.

Warm lobster salad with mango

• Wash and gently dry the purslane and coriander. Refrigerate until needed. Tie the bouqet garni herbs into a bundle.

• Bring a large pan of salted water to the boil with the bouquet garni. Add the lobsters and cook for 10–15 minutes. Remove and extract the flesh while the lobsters are still warm. Keep the meat warm between 2 plates.

• Peel the ripe mango. Cut one quarter into small cubes and thinly slice the rest. Peel the small green mango and cut into small cubes. Very finely chop the kaffir lime leaf and half of the coriander.

• In a small pan, combine the olive oil, lime juice and sweet and sour sauce. Heat gently, then add the chopped lime leaf, coriander and all the mango cubes. Season with salt and pepper and keep warm over a pan of simmering water.

• Lightly steam the lobster meat to warm. Slice the tail. Divide the purslane and remaining coriander between 4 plates. Top with the mango cubes and lobster and drizzle with the warm lime juice mixture. Serve immediately.

Serves 4
Preparation: 20 minutes
Cooking time:
20 minutes

2 large handfuls purslane, or spinach, leaves
½ bunch of fresh coriander
1 bouquet garni (parsley, sprig of thyme and bay leaf)
2 lobsters, about 400 g (14 oz) each
1 firm, ripe mango
1 small green mango
1 kaffir lime leaf
6 tablespoons olive oil
2 tablespoons lime juice
1 tablespoon sweet and sour sauce
salt and freshly ground pepper

White vegetable salad with smoked haddock

• Cut the haddock into thin slices and arrange on a plate. Pour over half of the lemon juice and 1 tablespoon of the olive oil. Refrigerate.

• Trim the spring onions and thinly slice the white parts. Peel and thinly slice the turnips. Trim the chicory and remove any blemished leaves, then wash and cut into thin slices. Wash and dry the dill, then snip with scissors.

• For the vinaigrette: whisk together the walnut oil and the remaining olive oil and lemon juice. Stir in the dill and season with salt and pepper.

• Put the whipping cream in a bowl, stir in the allspice and beat until it holds firm peaks. Refrigerate until needed.

• Heat the sunflower oil in a small frying pan. When hot, add the turnip slices and cook until golden and crispy, about 3 minutes. Transfer to kitchen paper to drain.

• Combine the onions, chicory and vinaigrette and toss well. Divide between 4 plates and top each with equal amounts of marinated haddock, turnip crisps and savoury whipped cream. Serve immediately.

Serves 4
Preparation: 20 minutes
Cooking time: 3 minutes

450 g (1 lb) smoked haddock
8 tablespoons lemon juice
3 tablespoons olive oil
1 bunch of large spring onions
1 bunch of small purple-tinged turnips
3 chicory heads
½ bunch of fresh dill
1 tablespoon walnut oil
200 ml (7 fl oz) whipping cream
2 pinches ground allspice
150 ml (5 fl oz) sunflower oil
salt and freshly ground pepper

Warm potato salad with truffles

• Wash the potatoes and boil in their skins until tender, about 20 minutes. Wipe and peel the truffles. Put the truffle peelings in the olive oil to infuse for at least 15 minutes. Cut the truffles into thin slices, cover and set aside.

• For the vinaigrette: whisk together the vinegar and infused olive oil. Season with salt and pepper.

• Peel the potatoes while still warm and slice into rounds. Gently toss the potato slices with the truffles and vinaigrette. Cover with clingfilm and set aside at room temperature for 20 minutes.

• Meanwhile, wash the lamb's lettuce and pat dry. Serve the potato salad with the lamb's lettuce.

Note: it only takes a few shavings of truffle peel to flavour any oil. Do not use too many, or leave too long in the oil. If using preserved truffles, add the liquid to the vinaigrette for extra flavour.

Serves 4
Preparation: 20 minutes
Cooking time:
20 minutes
Steeping time:
15 minutes
Resting time:
20 minutes

450 g (1 lb) potatoes

100 g (3½ oz) fresh or preserved truffles

About 300 ml (10½ fl oz) olive oil

1 tablespoon sherry vinegar

2 handfuls lamb's lettuce (mâche)

salt and freshly ground pepper

index of recipes